DISCUSSION PAPER 66

ELECTORAL DEMOCRATISATION
IN POST-CIVIL WAR GUINEA-BISSAU 1999–2008

LARS RUDEBECK

NORDISKA AFRIKAINSTITUTET, UPPSALA 2011

Indexing terms:
Guinea-Bissau
Post-conflict reconstruction
Democratization
Elections
Political parties
Political participation
Democracy
Political conditions
Economic conditions

Language checking: Peter Colenbrander

ISSN 1104-8417

ISBN 978-91-7106-706-7

© The author and Nordiska Afrikainstitutet 2011

Production: Byrå4

Print on demand, Lightning Source UK Ltd.

Contents

Foreword

This Discussion Paper provides a theoretical exploration of the challenges facing democracy and development in Africa, drawing on the case of Guinea-Bissau, recently recovering from a decade of violent conflict and political instability. In critically examining a phenomenon the paper conceptualises as 'democracy without development,' the author demonstrates the 'limitations of democratic constitutionalism, epitomised by general multiparty elections.' It is argued that democratic constitutionalism weakly rooted in the political, economic and cultural structures of societies is most likely to result in instability and underdevelopment. This implies that liberal democracy fails to deliver equality in practice in societies characterised by mass poverty and wide inequalities. This is the backdrop to the case study of the attempts at post-conflict democratisation in Guinea-Bissau between 1998 and 2009. By analysing the cycle of military intervention, political assassination and instability, the paper demonstrates the inability of electoral democracy to address the everyday survival challenges that the people face, and their aspirations. The author also explores the role of the international aid, noting that it has fuelled dependence and undermined Guinea-Bissau's autonomy. In seeking ways to resolve the dilemma of 'democracy without development,' the author notes that the real challenge lies in making 'needs' and 'resources' meet, a process that would require political, economic and cultural transformation. This Discussion Paper provides its readers with a profound theoretical and empirical background for understanding the challenges of democratisation and development in one of West Africa's most fragile post-conflict countries.

Cyril Obi
Senior Researcher
The Nordic Africa Institute

Acronyms

AD	*Acção Democrática*/Democratic action
APU	*Aliança Popular Unida*/Popular united alliance
FCG-SD	*Fórum Cívico Guineense – Social Democracia*/Guinean civic forum – social democracy
FDS	*Frente Democrática Social*/Democratic social front
FLING	*Frente da Libertacão Nacional da Guiné*/Guinea's national liberation front
HDI	*Human Development Index*
LIPE	*Liga Guinense de Protecção e Desenvolvimento Ecológico*/Guinean league for ecological protection and development
MDG	*Movimento Democrático Guineense*/Guinean Democratic Movement
PAIGC	*Partido Africano da Independência da Guiné e Cabo Verde*/African party for the independence of Guinea and Cape Verde
PDSG	*Partido Democrático Socialista Guineense*/Guinean democratic socialist party
PMP	*Partido do Manifesto do Povo*/Party of the people's manifesto
PND	*Partido da Nova Democracia*/Party of the new democracy
PRID	*Partido Republicano da Independência e do Desenvolvimento*/Republican party for independence and development
PRP	*Partido da Renovação e Progresso*/Party for renewal and progress
PRS	*Partido da Renovação Social*/Party for social renewal
PSD	*Partido Social Democrata*/Social democratic party
PS	*Partido Socialista*/Socialist party
PU	*Plataforma Unida*/United platform
PT	*Partido do Trabalho*/Party of labour
PUN	*Partido da União Nacional*/Party of national union
PUSD	*Partido Unido Social Democrata*/United social democratic party
RGB	*Resistência da Guiné-Bissau*/Guinea-Bissau's resistance
RGB/MB	*Resistência da Guiné-Bissau - Movimento Bâ-Fatá*/Guinea-Bissau's resistance – Bâ-Fatá-movement
UE	*União Eleitoral*/Electoral union
UM	*União para a Mudança*/Union for change
UNDP	*União Nacional para o Desenvolvimento e Progresso*/National union for development and progress

Electoral democratisation: an introductory overview

Viewed in broad historical perspective (Rudebeck 2002 and 2003) *constitution-alism,* as rule by law, *without* democracy, has existed for centuries in the so-called Western historical experience. But what I like to call 'the *democratisation* of constitutionalism' (2001:20; 2002(a):175) in the 'West' (or 'North') through universal suffrage and civil rights for all is a recent outcome of growing popular influence and power in society. Nowhere does it date further back at the national level than to the second half of the 19th century.

In the even more recent processes of democratisation in the postcolonial 'South,' beginning in the late 1980s, *democratic constitutionalism* – epitomised most vividly by *general multiparty elections* – has tended to come as a ready-made package, largely from the outside and above, straight into societies marked by quite limited popular sovereignty or citizen autonomy. Consequently, democratisation, although welcomed by the people, is still often weakly rooted in the institutional structure of the societies concerned, as illustrated not least by recent 'post-conflict' situations.[1] Electoral democratisation alone does not ensure democracy.

The case of Guinea-Bissau is one of several illuminating examples of this, including a clear 'post-conflict' situation. What does it tell us? This is the question dealt with in this paper. First, however, a brief outline is provided of the theoretical argument used to link the concepts of democratisation and development at the abstract level and also to structure the concrete empirical presentation on Guinea-Bissau.[2]

Democracy, democratisation and development

There is a fundamental and persistent dilemma in democratic theory springing from the tension between democracy conceptualised as a form of rule characterised by *universal suffrage, regular elections and basic civil rights* and democracy conceptualised as *political equality in actual practice.*[3]

The first definition or conceptualisation, that most often applied by modern

---

1. Stressing the notion of 'post-conflict' democratisation risks obscuring the fact that democratisation is almost always conflictual. The notion may still be useful in turning our attention to policy issues of interest to the so-called international community and also to those directly affected in their daily lives by the conflicts preceding the post-conflict stage as well as the destructive chaos of that stage itself.

2. Very special thanks to Bill Turpin, Bissau, regularly providing the author with electoral documents and Bissau newspapers throughout the 2000-06 period, thus making the writing of this paper possible.

3. For my views on this, see, for instance, Rudebeck 2002 and 2003. The first four paragraphs of this section have been extracted with only slight modifications from 2003, pp. 6–7.

political scientists, is often called the *minimalist*, because it is an operational definition *limiting* democracy to its essential *institutional* – constitutional, procedural – manifestations. The second definition or conceptualisation certainly views democracy as including the institutionalisation of political equality and basic freedoms, but it does not stop there. According to the second view, democracy can be meaningfully grasped and conceptualised only *in the context of its own realisation in actual practice*. How does the system work? Who is represented in what ways? Is political power equalised in ways that are meaningful to the citizens concerned? Such questions are integral to the concept of democracy, according to the second view.

My own striving is to practise the second view without giving up on democratic constitutionalism. This means a two-dimensional conceptualisation of democracy: *democratic constitutionalism* and *popular sovereignty/citizen autonomy* as *two distinct but linked dimensions of actually existing democracy and ongoing processes of democratisation*.

Where both dimensions are present, we are faced with deep, broad and 'substantial'[4] democracy, which can be expected to be more sustainable and durably legitimate than democracy limited to the constitutional level, not least by creating power entitlements for citizens that make it possible for them to assume responsibility for their own country's development.

Depending on the context, democracy in its minimalist sense may or may not be correlated with 'development,' whether in the descriptive sense of growth in GNP and related indicators or in a structural sense, linking needs to possibilities and resources. The broader, deeper or more substantial democracy is, however, the more it is logically linked to needs-based development, that is 'development' in a structural sense, viewed as a process whereby existing possibilities are used to satisfy legitimate needs. Any such development requires that the needs to be satisfied be defined and decided upon, which is where political power is crucial. If the needs in question are those of the majority of the people, or even needs and interests common to entire countries and peoples, then the chances they will be prioritised in definition and implementation are greatest if they are democratically decided upon, in a process characterised by at least a measure of power equalisation. Those people, in many cases the great majority, whose elementary needs have to be at least partially met for any stability to be achieved, have to have some substantial political power.

From a conceptual perspective, *democracy* is a *structure of power*. Democrati-

---

4.   This is the term used by Törnquist 2002, pp. 29 and 31, where he conceptualises 'substantial' democracy as follows: 'Substantial democracy "only" means that the conventional democratic rules of the game ... are both fair and applied in vital sectors of society ...' (p. 29).

sation is a *process*. *Democratisation*, in the substantial sense, thus turns out to be equal to *political development*.

Specifying the meaning of *'development'* in greater depth is, as we know, a tricky, in fact a never-ending task (cf., Rudebeck 1991 and 2003). For the purposes of this paper, it will be dealt with in relation to our empirical case, to which we now turn.

Breakdown and subsequent 'normality' in Guinea-Bissau, 1998–2006[5]

War, transition and return to constitutional democracy, 1998–2000

The last few years of the 1990s were violent ones in Guinea-Bissau. Although the ruling regime had been legally democratic since 1994, it was hardly legitimate within its own society. Civil and regional war erupted in June 1998, breaking the relative peace that had lasted since independence in 1974. Despite support from several thousand soldiers sent mainly by neighbouring Senegal and Guinea (Conakry), internal resistance forced President João Bernardo 'Nino' Vieira to abdicate in May 1999. Under the leadership of a transitional government, the country returned to constitutional democracy through general elections in November 1999 (parliamentary and presidential) and January 2000 (second-round presidential).

The former opposition party, PRS gained a parliamentary majority and ousted PAIGC, the pre-independence liberation movement and Guinea-Bissau's ruling party from 1974 to 1998. The presidential election was also won by the opposition candidate Kumba Yalá, who gained 69 per cent of the national vote in the second round. He was installed as new president for a five-year period in February 2000 (Rudebeck 2001 and 2004).

Democracy without development

The new democratically constituted regime proved unable to deal with Guinea-Bissau's development problems. The country's economy stagnated or regressed and the quality of life of the people deteriorated in rural as well as urban areas. The HDI ranking remained close to the bottom (see below). Governments were moving in and out of office. There was strong dissatisfaction among the military, who were owed unpaid salaries. True enough, democratic institutions were in place, but critical journalists and newspapers as well as independent judges and opposition politicians were frequent victims of repression by the president, the

---

5. Our empirical analysis ends largely with the 2005 presidential contest and its political aftermath until March 2006. Subsequent events and developments in Guinea-Bissau, until the moment of putting a final touch to the text (November 2008), so far follow the same pattern as emerging from that analysis, and thus confirms it. Cf. note 7.

security police and the courts. The question of a 'truth and reconciliation commission' on the South African model to deal with the wounds of conflict was raised, but never moved beyond the stage of superficial discussion. In sum, during these first few years following the civil war the gap between state and society appeared as wide as ever and perhaps even to be widening, in spite of electoral democratisation.

Military putsch, September 2003

On 14 September 2003, Kumba Yalá, the president elected in 2000, was deposed in a bloodless military putsch – fairly quickly but somewhat reluctantly accepted by the 'international community' as inevitable under the circumstances. The military appointed the businessman Henrique Rosa as provisional president. A National Transition Council made up of 56 members (25 military representatives, 23 persons appointed the political parties and 8 by civil society organisations) became the provisional parliament. On 18 September 2003 a provisional constitutional agreement, a 'mini-constitution' called the Political Transition Charter/*Carta de Transição Política* (2003), was signed by the members of the transitional council.

Second post-civil war parliamentary election March 2004

After a quite peaceful constitutional transition, regular parliamentary elections were held on 28 March 2004, resulting in the return to power of PAIGC. Kumba Yalá's PRS came second. A new government based on the 45 parliamentary seats out of 100 gained by PAIGC was installed on 12 May 2004 under the premiership of PAIGC Secretary-General Carlos Gomes Jr. Initially, this government was also supported by PRS (35 seats) and by UM, a coalition of small parties that gained two parliamentary seats (*Lusa* 24 May 2004).

The consolidation of democracy in the country, however, proved elusive. In October 2004, a military mutiny resulting in the murder of the commander-in-chief and another high-ranking officer upset the fragile political balance in Guinea-Bissau.

Second post-civil war presidential election 2005

Furthermore, presidential elections were also approaching. In terms of the *Carta de Transição Política*, the first round was scheduled for no later than 8 May 2005, one year after the inauguration of the parliament elected in 2004. Agreeing on the election date was complicated by the need to update the census, a politically sensitive operation that also required financing (with aid money, underlining Guinea-Bissau's extreme dependence on aid) as well as transparency.

In the end, the first round of the presidential election took place on 19 June

2005. The election-day process was credibly deemed free and fair by observers and commentators, internal and external. The prelude, however, had been conflictual as well as questionable.

PAIGC's candidate, Malam Bacai Sanhá, backed by a parliamentary majority, had unexpectedly had to face two strong challengers, who managed to enter the contest late in the day. One was Kumba Yalá, the very person forced to resign from the presidency in September 2003, less than two years earlier. The other, and more potent, opponent was no less than João Bernardo 'Nino' Vieira, president of Guinea-Bissau from 1980 to 1999, who had been forced to flee his palace for the Portuguese embassy in Bissau on 7 May 1999, leaving for political asylum in Portugal one month later. To the surprise of many (but not all), Vieira returned for a few days from Portuguese asylum in early April 2005 in an air force helicopter belonging to neighbouring (Conakry) to visit his supporters and his mother and to register as a voter (*Lusa* 7–12 April 2005; *Gazeta de Notícias* 15 April 2005; *Nô Pintcha* 20 May 2005).

On the deadline for registration, 19 April, the Guinea-Bissau supreme court published a list of 21 people who had registered as candidates for the presidential election, among them João Bernardo Vieira, who intended to run as an independent (*Lusa* 19 April 2005; *Diário Bissau* 22 April 2005) and Kumba Yalá. On 10 May, the court finally announced its approval of 19 of the candidacies, including Vieira's and Kumba Yalá's (*Lusa* 10 May 2005; *Nô Pintcha* 12 May 2005), although both had been vigorously disputed on juridical grounds. In both cases, the arguments turned on the presumed constitutional legality/illegality of allowing citizens who had renounced their claims to the presidency to run anew. Yalá claimed that although he had signed an act of resignation and withdrawal, in reality he had been forced to do so (*Gazeta de Notícias* 22 April 2005; *Diário Bissau* 29 April 2005), while Vieira's main juridical argument seems to have been the length of time since his resignation in June 1999 (*Lusa* April-May 2005; *Gazeta de Notícias* 3 May 2005; *Kansaré*, 16 May 2005).

Paradoxical outcome of presidential election, June-July-October 2005

Whatever the constitutional and political arguments for or against his participation, on election day, 19 June 2005, 'Nino' Vieira did in fact run as an independent candidate against the PAIGC, which he had served for over 40 years until 1999. Kumba Yalá ran as the official candidate of his PRS party. All told, 13 of the 19 candidates approved by the supreme court ran. Six chose to withdraw for various reasons. As expected, Malam Bacai Sanhá, backed by PAIGC and its parliamentary majority, won the first round, winning 34 per cent of the reported vote. Vieira came second (27 per cent) and Yalá third (24 per cent).[6]

---

6.   See introductory note in the *Appendix* on different ways of calculating these percentages.

With no candidate securing more than 50 per cent, the way was opened for a dramatic second round between the first two on 24 July 2005. This time, in spite (or because) of the circumstances, the official winner was 'Nino' Vieira with 51.1 per cent of the reported vote against 46.5 for Sanhá. Kumba Yalá had recommended to his supporters that they vote for 'Nino,' as had the former prime minister in the 1999 transitional government Francisco Fadul (*Lusa* 22 June 2005, 5 July 2005). The victory was contested by the loser and by the ruling party, which accused Vieira of cheating. Finally, on 1 October 2005, Vieira was reinstated as president of the republic in a charged political atmosphere (*Lusa* September-October 2005; *Diário Bissau* 29 September 2005; *Baloba Notícias* 5 October 2005) – six years, four months and three weeks after being chased from the presidential palace by his own army and by popular revolt.

Shifting coalitions and continuing instability

When it became evident in early 2005 that the presidential election might not be the easy victory hoped for by PAIGC, never-appeased tensions within the majority party surfaced in several ways, not least in the National Assembly itself. For instance, the leader of PAIGC parliamentary group, Cipriano Cassamá, whom the prime minister had vainly tried to have suspended from that position (*Lusa* 13 January 2005, 5 February 2005) came out against the PAIGC government in favour of a general amnesty that would also cover various criminal acts of which João Bernardo Vieira was suspected (*Lusa* 2 March 2005), though never formally accused by a prosecutor. Cassamá was one of several prominent PAIGC politicians and parliamentary representatives critical of the government formed by their own party and who, later, even supported 'Nino' for president against the PAIGC candidate (*Lusa* 13 September 2005). Another member of this group was the former PAIGC vice president, Aristides Gomes.

At the end of October 2005, Vieira himself, as newly appointed president, intervened in PAIGC's internal struggle by dismissing Carlos Gomes Jr. from the premiership and installing the latter's rival Aristides Gomes (*Lusa*, 29 October 2005, 2 November 2005) as new prime minister. During the following months, the new government was able to maintain itself in power with the help of defectors from the PAIGC parliamentary group, originally consisting of 45 deputies. The National Assembly's approval, finally, on 16 March 2006 of the programme of Aristides Gomes's government was a political victory for the president. The only opposing votes were those of the 36 remaining PAIGC deputies (*Lusa* 16 March 2006). Political instability continued, however. One year later, Aristides Gomes was forced to resign as prime minister after a parliamentary no-confidence vote. He was succeeded by Martinho N'Dafa Cabi, a PAIGC member but assumed to be more technocratic and less involved in partisan conflict (*Lusa* 21

March 2007, 9 April 2007, 11 April 2007). He in turn lasted till August 2008, when Carlos Correia, an old PAIGC veteran, was appointed prime minister (*Lusa* 12 August 2008). But as early as February 2008, the major party in the coalition, PAIGC, had already withdrawn its support for the prime minister (*Lusa* 29 February 2008), who thenceforward had to depend on the president. Thus the period as a whole was marked by stalemated political conflict between president and parliament, as well as within and between major political parties.

On 16 November 2008, parliamentary elections were again held in Guinea-Bissau. Initial reports were that election day passed off in peaceful and orderly fashion, resulting in a convincing two-thirds majority for PAIGC (*Lusa* 16–21 November 2008). At first glance, this outcome seemed to herald a measure of political stability under the renewed premiership of Carlos Gomes Jr. However, less than a week after the election, during the early hours of 23 November 2008, the president of the republic barely survived an armed attack on his residence by nine sailors from his own navy (*Lusa* 23–26 November 2008). Thus, there is little reason to expect substantial political change to flow from the election.[7]

What can be learnt?

The above is an outline of an infinitely complex web of political events unfolding in a society traumatised by civil war on top of permanently promised but never-arriving 'development,' whether pre- or post-conflict, and in spite of democratisation.

What can be learnt from all this? I will try in particular to open up a discussion of possible linkages between electoral democratisation and development.[8]

---

7.   On 27 November, the National Election Commission (CNE) announced the 'definite' results, according to which PAIGC gained a comfortable two-thirds majority in the National Assembly with 67 of the 100 seats (*Lusa* 28 November 2008). Former president Kumba Yalá's PRS gained 28. Altogether 19 political parties took part, but besides the two mentioned only three more gained representation, with three seats for PRID and one each for PND and a coalition of minor groupings. On 28 November 2008, PRS, the major opposition party, and PND, which gained only one seat in the 16 November election, presented a joint petition to the supreme court challenging the results on the grounds that fraud had been observed. They demanded that the elections in several districts be either re-run or that the votes be recounted (*Lusa* 28 November 2008). If successful, this move could result in PAIGC losing the constitutionally important two-thirds majority in the National Assembly by losing one or more seats to the opposition. On 28 November, furthermore, PRS announced its overall rejection of the results announced by the CNE (*Lusa* 28 November 2008). So far there is nothing but rumour about the forces or groups behind the assault on the president.

8.   This is continuation of work I have been pursuing for decades using the West-African case of Guinea-Bissau for empirical and theoretical deepening (e.g., Rudebeck 1991, 2001, 2002(b), 2004, 2006(b), 2008).

The elections

As we have seen, within a space of nine years between November 1999 and November 2008, as many as seven national-level general elections took place in Guinea-Bissau (counting the two rounds in the two presidential elections separately):

- 28 November 1999, National Assembly election
- 28 November 1999, first round presidential election
- 16 January 2000, second round presidential election
- 28 March 2004, National Assembly election
- 19 June 2005, first round presidential election
- 24 July 2005, second round presidential election
- 16 November 2008, National Assembly election

The outcomes of the 1999–2005 elections are summarised in tables 1–6 in the Appendix at the end of the text.

Close reading of the tables, supplemented with other information, reveals or indicates many things about hotly debated issues such as the role of electoral politics in intensifying or transcending ethnic and religious divisions in society; the great number of political parties and presidential candidates; and the vagueness of, or absence of, ideological divisions between the parties. Let me offer a few observations on these matters.

Malam Bacai Sanha, leading PAIGC national politician and major presidential candidate in both 1999/2000 and 2005, belongs to a southern minority ethnic group, the Beafada, most of whom are Moslem, as is Sanha himself. About 40 per cent of the Guinean population are held to be Moslem. Still, in both elections, many Moslem voters preferred Kumba Yalá or 'Nino' Vieira, both non-Moslem and leaning syncretistically towards Christianity/animism.

Kumba Yalá belongs to the major Balanta group, which makes up about 25 per cent of the population. It is easy to verify that his presidency signified the ascension of many Balanta to high political and military office. It is also true that Yalá himself in 1999/2000 (and his PRS, both then and in 2004, although not shown in the tables) did extremely well or well in predominantly Balanta areas. Still, Kumba Yalá in 1999/2000 also drew many votes even from several Moslem areas.

The dramatic 2005 presidential contest, which in the end pitted two veteran PAIGC (ex-PAIGC in Vieira's case) politicians against each other, is similarly illustrative and inconclusive as regards the ethno-religious factor. 'Nino' Vieira belongs to the Papel ethnic group, which is predominant in the area northwest of the capital Bissau, but he is pre-eminently a *national* Guinean politician, like

Malam Bacai Sanha. Their election results in both rounds indicate that both re-cruited voters across ethno-religious lines. Bacai Sanha's vote in particular was quite evenly distributed over the country. Even so, 'Nino' scored as high as 87 per cent in the Biombo 'homeland' of the Papel. Furthermore, it is said by insightful local observers, although not so easy to verify statistically, that Bacai Sanha's Mos-lem religion was decisive in depriving him of final victory on 24 July 2005, not least by turning urbanised Bissau voters otherwise sceptical of Vieira against him.

It is difficult to say with any certainty whether these observations support (or do not) the notion that electoral democratisation is likely to aggravate eth-no-religious tensions in society, even to the extent of obstructing development. Certainly the 'Balanta factor' and ethno-religious factors in general are potent in Guinean politics, but so are many other factors. The latter, furthermore, blend with the former, sometimes inseparably.

It is notable, too, that the 1998–99 civil war, was not primarily an ethnic war. The leader of the forces challenging the pre-1999 regime of 'Nino' Vieira was the military man Ansumane Mané, a deeply Moslem ethnic Mandinga (around 15 per cent of the Guinean population are Mandinga), originally of Gambian nationality.[9] Even so, the revolt certainly had overwhelming support among the Balanta of Guinea-Bissau, who are strictly non-Moslem.[10]

As also seen from the tables, the number of political parties and presiden-tial candidates taking part in elections is very high for a small country with a population of about 1.5 million people. It is not possible, however, to distin-guish between the political parties of Guinea-Bissau by studying their party pro-grammes. These and similar documents demonstrate clearly that all the parties claim to stand for democracy, justice and human rights, as well as for a socially responsible market economy. Any discernible differences tend to concern social and cultural/ethnic belonging, sources of financing, historical ties between lead-ers and supporters and the personal qualities of leaders. The same goes for the presidential candidates (see Rudebeck 2001:48–62.)

Whatever can be said about the parties, the tables of *Appendix 1* reflect the fact that in 1999–2005 electoral democracy was intensively evident in Guinea-Bissau. Elections have been held, citizens have gone to vote in considerable num-bers, politicians have moved in and out of office, elected parliamentarians have shifted their loyalties in ways perhaps not expected by their original supporters, international observers have given their stamp of approval, sometimes with some hesitation, but still. The problem, thus, is not lack of electoral democracy.

---

9. Ansumane Mané was subsequently killed in unclear circumstances, most probably mur-dered by the armed forces of Kumba Yalá's regime, on 30 November 2003. See Rudebeck 2001, pp. 96–98.

10. See Rudebeck 2001, pp. 28–30, for further comments on the origins of the 1988–99 conflict.

On the other hand, it would be very wrong to conclude illogically, as some may be tempted to do, that electoral democracy is a root cause of the problems of Guinea-Bissau. It is simply an insufficient solution to the kind of societal condition epitomised by rank 175 in the HDI of 2007–08, just two places above the bottom rank, as we shall now see.

Never-arriving development

As far as countrywide levels of 'development' are concerned, the UN Development Programme's HDI provides us with a composite quantitative measure of unsurpassed validity. In the following table, Guinea-Bissau's pre- and post-conflict HDI scores (running from zero to one) and rankings are shown. The 2007–08 score indicates no real improvement over pre- and immediate post-conflict levels. For the Guinean people, both the absence of change and the reality of the extremely low absolute level are alarming, to say the least.

HDI score and rank of Guinea-Bissau, rank of country at bottom level
(various years)

Year	Guinea-Bissau HDI-score	Guinea-Bissau rank	Bottom rank all
2000 (1998 data)	0.331	169	174
2003 (2001 data)	0.373	166	175
2007/2008 (various estimates)	0.374	175	177

Sources: UN Development Programme, Human Development Report 2000, table 1, p. 160; Human Development Report 2003, table 1, p. 240; Human Development Report 2007/2008, table 1, p. 232.

Concretely, Guinea-Bissau's 2007/2008 HDI score, based on best available data, represents an estimated average life expectancy at birth of 46 years; a roughly estimated adult literacy rate of 45 per cent; an estimated overall combined primary, secondary and tertiary school enrolment rate of 37 per cent; and an estimated average per capita purchasing power of 827 purchasing-power adjusted $ US. The latter is 16 per cent of the average for the world's 'developing countries' and no more than 2.8 per cent of the OECD average. Behind or below these overall figures there are of course all kinds of more specific variations.

It should be remembered that generally HDI variables are rather long-term and slow to change, meaning that specific improvements in limited respects will not be easily registered by the index, especially not within a few years.

Democracy, democratisation and development – in the concrete

I have attempted in two recent articles (2004, 2008) to highlight the implications of democratisation by drawing on the case study of the village of Kandjadja in northern Guinea-Bissau, which I have had occasion to visit and re-visit many times since 1976, including the more recent 'post-conflict' situation since 1998-99. Much of the following draws on that work, in which I note significantly, among other things, that 'civil society had been activated without becoming democratised' (2004:15).

Private and public in politics

The problem of democratisation at the national level resulting in civil society at local level being activated rather than democratised is obviously not restricted to Guinea-Bissau. It has general relevance. When the local political process is focused on and reaches into family and personal interests of survival and reproduction, it will very easily take the form of 'patron-client relationships' rather than democratic organisation. Both citizens and leaders take advantage of whatever opportunities are available to them to promote their short-term interests. As far as the citizens are concerned, in situations of material poverty, this is principally a question of day-to-day survival; while for the politicians it is more a question of accessing power and resources. As long as the citizens cannot discern any concrete reasons to assume that public, collective, action might actually help them survive and improve their lives, the likelihood is high that they will continue to turn to their patrons, even under the guise of the constitutionally democratic system or through various civil society activities – not so much because they trust those patrons but because they do not see any realistic alternatives.

This looks like an impasse, at least in the short run. In the somewhat longer run, however, the negative dynamics of such a situation are not sustainable. Both the development necessary for people to survive in acceptable ways and their readiness, as well as capacity, to support the patrons' power are undermined. The example of the village of Kandjadja is instructive – mainly by clearly demonstrating how little the local people get in return for their political support, but perhaps also by suggesting certain limits to their patience, as shown for instance by a decline in voting support for PAIGC between 1994 and 1999/2000, however modest in national comparison.[11] Still, so far, the self-perceived short-

---

11. The decline for PAIGC did not continue in the 28 March 2004 parliamentary election, however. On the contrary, the Kandjadja voters on that occasion conformed to the overall national trend of showing lack of trust in the first non-PAIGC government ever. Thus, in 2004 PAIGC scored 257 votes out of 363 valid votes (71 per cent) in the village of Kandjadja, as against 172 out of 432 (40 per cent) in 1999. Thus, support for PAIGC was even higher in 2004 than in 1994 (information on 2004 voting outcome collected in Kandjadja on 29 June 2007.)

term interest of the villagers has not incited them to new forms of politicisation, beyond participating in multiparty elections.[12]

Democratisation and control over developmental resources

The above conclusion on politicisation in Kandjadja over the last decade brings up the problem of democratisation and development seen together, as they materialise in Guinea-Bissau and other countries marked by mass poverty. Abstractly formulated, this is the key developmental problem of how to *make needs and resources meet*. For that problem to be resolved, needs must be defined and existing resources must be put to use. This is a three-dimensional task, as it involves not only economy and politics, but also culture. The more equally distributed the power to define needs and to control relevant resources is, the more democratic, by definition, is the society in question, and the greater the chance that existing resources will be used in accordance with the developmental needs of the many. Culture may either facilitate or obstruct this process. This goes to the core of the conceptual theme of democracy and democratisation in relation to development.

Democratisation and women's representation

The link is close between development and the gender dimension of democratisation. One question among many in this large complex of theoretical and empirical issues is the effects of electoral democratisation upon women's representation in the political process. A simple indicator is the proportion of women elected to parliament. It is striking that in Guinea-Bissau democratisation coincided with a considerable reduction of that proportion. The table given below is unambiguous in this regard. Although I do not here present data for other countries and situations, we have no reason to believe that Guinea-Bissau would be unique in this respect.[13]

The last undemocratically elected parliament, before democratisation reached Guinea-Bissau in the early 1990s, was that of 1989. In the National Assembly elected that year, there were 30 women deputies out of a total of 150, or 20 per

---

12. Revisiting Kandjadja on 29 June 2007, I did, however, learn that the villagers themselves had in 2005 started a private school offering the first three grades of primary school to substitute for the state school that had been closed down in 1989 and had never reopened since. The employment of a teacher for the new community-run school was financed by each family putting in CFA 350 (0.53 euro) per month and child. This village initiative can be seen as a sign of substantial democratisation of civil society at the local level. The school was still operating in the autumn of 2008.

13. Taking an historical view, it is known, for example, that the introduction of female suffrage in countries such as Sweden and Germany after the First World War was statistically correlated with successes scored by conservative parties that had been opposed to democratisation in this form (Tingsten 1963:36 ff.).

cent. Then, as earlier, the parliament had been filled on the basis of a top-down method by indirect one-party elections, in which the voters first appointed regional assemblies from PAIGC's one-party lists and where the members of those assemblies in turn selected from among themselves the persons who were to sit in parliament. It is not surprising that the leadership, if it so wanted, was able to produce a fairly large proportion of women in such a process. When the process became freer, the proportion of women in the National Assembly declined rapidly to 9 per cent in 1994 and, in the 1999 election, to less than 8 per cent.[14] As seen in the table below, the proportion has not changed so far during the post-civil war period.

The participation of a woman-led political party (FCG-SD) in the multiparty elections did not have any apparent effect on the number of women elected to political office. Nor is it likely to have had any noticeable effect on the overall participation of women as voters, considering FCG-SD's meagre results from a statistical point of view. Quite possibly the participation of FCG-SD as a political party and Antonieta Rosa Gomes as its presidential candidate on three different occasions from 1999 to 2005 might have had long-term attitudinal effects in Guinean society, although these cannot be known on the basis of electoral data alone.

One certain conclusion to be drawn from the comparison presented in the table is that the transition from undemocratic to democratic election procedure does not, by itself, guarantee a larger proportion of women in the National Assembly. Another conclusion is that the 'post-conflict' situation did not bring any statistical change in this regard in Guinea-Bissau. These are conclusions, I think, that merit attention in the wider context of democratisation and development.

Proportion of women among the total number of members elected to the National Assembly in 1989, 1994, 1999 and 2004

	absolute figures	%
1989	30/150	20
1994	9/100	9
1999	8/102	7.8
2004	10/100	10

Sources: Rudebeck 2001, p. 59; *Diário de Bissau*, 14 January 2000; *Diário Bissau*, 13 May 2004.

Power, culture and politics

As for the role of culture in politics, the crucial question is not whether the line of division between public and private is more diffuse in the political cultures of most African countries than, generally, in Western Europe and North America.

---

14. For detailed references in this regard on the 1994 and 1999 elections, see Rudebeck 2001, pp. 58–60.

It most probably is. The question is how far this kind of argument takes us in explaining lack of development. Patron-client relations and corruption certainly have not prevented economic development in other parts of the world, whether, for instance, historically in the West or in modern Asia.[15]

By concentrating – or appearing to concentrate – the explanatory effort on cultural variables, the question of *power* in society is avoided. But the distribution of political power is a key factor in development. Its equalisation is, furthermore, what democratisation is all about.

True enough, an inherited culture of client deference to patrons obviously supports unequal power and thus does not facilitate democratisation. But in accordance with Max Weber's classical sociological perspective, culture is more fruitfully analysed as the 'switchman' between interest and action than as an overall explanation of society as such. Culture provides values, images and frameworks for interpreting reality. But when necessary for daily survival, even democratically minded persons bow to patrons, however reluctantly. Likewise, powerful people whose cultural values are non-democratic may well agree to share inherited power if such is necessary to their political or even physical survival. Our explanatory efforts need to be pushed beyond the surface recognition of the factual existence of such behaviour. What material forces or interests and political structures actually obstruct democratisation? Why do democrats bend to bosses? Why do bosses sometimes accept democratisation?

Furthermore, control over many developmental resources important to Guinea-Bissau is in the hands of outside forces. Such inequality tends to be reinforced under the conditions of today's globalisation. It is even possible that control over developmental resources that actually *can* be locally and nationally managed under globalisation will long continue to escape most people in Guinea-Bissau and many other countries, in spite of democratisation.

If so, democracy will have turned out to be thinly and incompletely implemented. In most cases, this will not be because people, for cultural reasons, do not *want* power to be shared. Quite the reverse: the explanation will much more likely have to be sought in a complex structure of power that makes it excessively hard for Guineans in general and many others to make their developmental interests heard and seen, even within newly introduced democratic institutions, however much they would like to be able to do so. As long as this is the case, 'post-conflict' stability, except by repression, is likely to remain a dream.

---

15. Cf. the following methodological remark by Mahmood Mamdani (1996:295 note 2) on 'the mode of domination' as an explanatory variable: 'My point about clientelism is that it is more an effect of the form of power than an explanation of it.' My own related point is that the culture of clientelism does not *explain* clientelism: it *is* clientelism.

A note on the international context

I have earlier indicated (Rudebeck 2006) what can be learnt from the Guinea-Bissau experience since 1999 about the role of the 'international community' in 'post-conflict' democratisation. The following points are relevant (Ibid.:84–5):

- 'top-down' at the expense of 'bottom-up' has contributed significantly to the failure so far of post-conflict improvement and stabilisation;
- holding early parliamentary and presidential elections in November 1999, only six months after the end of civil war, was probably better than postponing the elections, as early elections in this case did concretise the meaning of democracy for many citizens;
- the situation of women as citizens changes or improves very slowly and unevenly, not visibly as a result of foreign aid, and is seemingly unaffected by the politically significant role once held by women in the 1963–74 anti-colonial struggle against Portugal.

These points were originally formulated before the 2005 presidential election, with its paradoxical outcome, had taken place. All indications are that they are equally relevant in 2008. Whatever stabilisation may be under way does not seem to carry the seeds of substantial improvement for the citizens in the short or medium run.

The 'solution'

The 'solution' to such impasses for the people of Guinea-Bissau would thus be to gradually break up the vertical patron-client structures of power and to create more democratic structures in their place by putting political pressure from below on the patrons, all the way up to the national level. This would have to involve horizontal self-organisation by people with similar developmental interests, rather than each one on his or her own linking up with better placed individuals running for office in an election, in the hope, for instance, of getting a job with cash remuneration in exchange for helping to mobilise voters. Most often that hope is never realised anyway.

If anything like the kind of horizontal self-organisation now indicated ever materialises, it will certainly come to *look like* a cultural revolution, in the sense of requiring that many customs and habits be changed. It is, however, more than doubtful that such self-organisation will be *brought about* (i.e., caused) by cultural change. In the theoretical perspective applied here, breaking up the vertical patron-client structures of power and creating more democratic structures in their place would simply be sheer survival necessity, *in spite* of age-old values and habits of patron-client dependence.

Conclusion

Guinea-Bissau, over nine years after the end of civil war, is still characterised by democratisation without development. An important contributory factor is the strong military, oversized for historical reasons but underpaid for financial reasons (when paid at all) and thus permanently dissatisfied and vulnerable to being influenced. Another critical factor is extreme dependence on international aid, even for such crucial but relatively inexpensive matters as the carrying out of elections. Such dependence constantly threatens to undermine the autonomy crucial to democracy.

The key underlying factor in Guinean society, however, is a very unequal power structure in which ordinary people have daily experience of underdevelopment and little or no control over the resources needed for substantial improvement of their lives. Democracy limited to electoral democracy will not resolve this. General elections are vital to democracy, but in societies marked by mass poverty, more is needed for democracy to make lasting sense (cf., Rudebeck 2002(b):126–7). There are no nationwide signs in Guinea-Bissau today of the horizontally organised pressure from below suggested above as crucial for democracy to become substantial.

I have, for instance, often asked myself what the difference would be between a West African village farmer struggling against poverty who does make use of the democratic institutions existing in his or her country and one who does not, beyond voting in elections. If citizens dared or found it useful to make use of their constitutional and democratic freedom of association to get together with others in, for instance, horizontally organised and functioning credit or farmers' associations, which could begin to loosen their members' dependence on various kinds of political and economic patrons, then deep or substantial democratisation would also, by definition, begin to take place, and 'development' would become a possibility.

References

Literature, reports, documents

Bangura, Yusuf, 2005, *Democracy, Responsiveness and Well-Being in Africa*. Paper to CODESRIA's 11th General Assembly, Maputo, Mozambique, 6-10 December 2005.

Boletim Oficial da República da Guiné-Bissau, no. 26, 1 July 2005, supplement 2, Bissau.

Carta de Transição Política, 2003, Bissau.

Comissão Nacional de Eleiçõe, 1999, Distribution of mandates by constituency, parliamentary election, 28. November 1999, Bissau, 9 December 1999.

—, Results of first round of presidential election, 28 November 1999, distribution of votes by candidates, regions and constituencies, Bissau, 11 December 1999.

—, 2000, Results of second round of presidential election, 16 January 2000, distribution of votes by candidates and regions, Bissau, 21 January 2000.

—, 2000, Results of first round of presidential election, 16 January 2000, distribution of votes by candidates and regions, Bissau, 25 January 2000.

—, 2005, Results of second round of presidential election, 24 July 2005, distribution of votes by candidates and regions, Bissau, 10 August 2005.

Ferrazzetta, D. Settimio, Bishop of Bissau, 1998, *'Bispo de Bissau pede ao povo para reagir,'* statement made during mass in Bissau cathedral, 9 August 1998, according to the Portuguesse news agency *Lusa*, 10 August 1998, internet: LGR0009 3 afr 535 335733.

Lusa: Agência de Notícias de Portugal, various dates and years. www.lusa.pt.

Mamdani, Mahmood, 1996, *Citizen and Subject. Contemporary Africa and the legacy of late colonialism*. Princeton: Princeton University Press.

Obi, Cyril, 2005, *Post-Conflict Transition, the State and Civil Society in Africa*. Project Description. Uppsala: Nordic Africa Institute.

Rudebeck, Lars, 1991, 'Conditions of people's development in postcolonial Africa,' in Rosemary E. Galli (ed.), *Rethinking the third world. Contributions toward a new conceptualization*. New York and London: Crane Russak, pp. 29–87.

—, 2001, *On Democracy's Sustainability. Transition in Guinea-Bissau*, Sida Studies No. 4, Stockholm: Sida (in Portuguese, somewhat revised, as *Colapso e Reconstrução Política na Guiné-Bissau 1998–2000. Um Estudo de Democratização Difícil*, Uppsala: Nordic Africa Institute, 2001).

—, 2002:a, 'Beyond Democratic Constitutionalism: On the twofold meaning of democracy and democratization,' *African Sociological Review* 6 (1), pp. 173–80.

—, 2002:b, 'Multi-Party Elections in Guinea-Bissau,' in Michael Cowen and Lisa Laakso (eds), *Multi-Party Elections in Africa*. London: James Currey, pp. 104–27.

—, 2003, 'Democracy as Actual Practice,' in Lars Rudebeck (ed.), *Democracy as Actual Practice: What Does Democracy Really Bring?* Utsikt mot utveckling, no. 20. Uppsala: Collegium for Development Studies, Uppsala University, pp. 5–15.

—, 2004, 'Democratisation and "Civil Society" in a West-African Village,' in *Decentralisation in Practice. Power, Livelihoods and Cultural Meaning in West Africa*, International Workshop Highlights, Uppsala, Sweden, 4–6 May 2004. London and Uppsala: IIED (International Institute for Environment and Development) and Department of Cultural Anthropology and Ethnology, Uppsala University (brochure + CD-ROM).

—, 2006:a, 'Reading Cabral on democracy,' *African Identities* 4 (1), pp. 89–98.

—, (ed.), 2006:b, *Violent Conflict and Democracy – Risks and Opportunities*. Utsikt mot utveckling, no. 27. Uppsala: Collegium for Development Studies, Uppsala University.

—, 2008, in publication, "'They Have Left Us in an Hole." Democratisation and Political Power in a West-African Village,' in thematic issue on decentralisation and citizen participation of *The APAD-Bulletin*, Euro-African Association for the Anthropology of Socil Change and development, Leiden and Uppsala.

Tingsten, Herbert, 1963 (1937), *Political Behaviour. Studies in election statistics* (Stockholm Economic Studies, 1937). Totowa NJ: Bedminster Press.

Törnquist, Olle, 2002, *Popular Development and Democracy. Case Studies with Rural Dimensions in the Philippines, Indonesia, and Kerala*. Geneva and Oslo: Centre for Development and the Environment (SUM), University of Oslo, in cooperation with UNRISD.

UNDP, (United Nations Development Programme), 1999, *Human Development Report 1999*. Oxford: Oxford University Press.

—, 2000, *Human Development Report 2000*. Oxford: Oxford University Press.

—, 2003, *Human Development Report 2003*. Oxford: Oxford University Press.

—, 2008, *Human Development Report 2007/2008*, New York. http://hdr.undp.org/en/media/hdr_20072008_tables.pdf

Newspapers

In preparing the present text, systematic reading of Lusa's reports from Bissau (listed above) has been supplemented with consultation of the following Bissau newspapers (which appear somewhat irregularly but still with admirable consistency and dedication, considering the conditions of work):

Baloba Notícias

Diário Bissau (formerly *Diário de Bissau*)

Fraskera

Gazeta de Notícias

Kansaré

Nô Pintcha (the name means 'forward' in Guinean Creole)

Appendix

Tables of general elections held in Guinea-Bissau, 1999–2005[16]

Table 1. Results, whole country, National Assembly (ANP) election 28 November 1999 (number of mandates and rounded-off percentage of total vote gained by each party)

	Mandates	% vote
PAIGC	24	15
RGB/MB	29	16
PRS	38	24
FDS	1	2
UM	3	7
LIPE	–	3
FLING	–	2
AD (PCD-FD)	3	4
PUSD	–	1 (1.1)
FCG-SD	–	1 (0.8)
PSD	3	5 (4.6)
UNDP	1	3 (3.3)
PRP	–	1 (0.9)
blank votes	–	13
not valid	–	4
Total	**102**	**100 %**
Total number of votes		**432,604**

Source: Comissão Nacional de Eleições, 9 December 1999 and 25 January 2000.

---

16. The percentages given in the tables have been calculated as shares of total vote, as opposed to shares of the total number of approved ('valid') votes, which is a common procedure, although somewhat misleading. As the latter, commonest, way of calculating was used in my sources, I have done some recalculations for my tables. The differences are small, however. The official percentages, for instance, for the second round of the 2005 presidential election were 52.35 per cent of the vote in favour of Joaô Bernardo Vieira and 47.65 for Malam Bacai Sanha, while table 6 below gives 51.1 versus 46.5.

The official statistics on which the tables are based only show participation *in relation to the number of registered* voters. Even real participation, however, calculated as *total vote/ estimated number of people of voting age*, had risen to over 70 per cent in 1999, according to my own rough estimates. The most recent such rates, similarly calculated, were 62 per cent for the 2004 parliamentary election (official rate 74.5), 61 for the first round of the 2005 presidential election (official 88) and 58 for the second round (official 79) (sources same as for tables 4, 5 and 6 below; details on manner of calculation in Rudebeck 2001, pp. 56–7.) These participation rates strengthen the impression of legitimacy in Guinea-Bissau for democratic elections.

Table 2. Results, whole country, first round of presidential election, 28 November 1999 (rounded-off percentage of total vote and numberof votes obtained by each candidate)

	% vote	Number of votes
Kumba Yalá (PRS)	34	143,996
Malam Bacai Sanhá (PAIGC)	20	86,724
Faustino Imbali (independent)	7	30,484
Fernando Gomes (independent)	6 (6.2)	26,049
João Tatis Sá (independent)	6 (5.8)	24,117
Abubacar Baldé (UNDP)	5	20,192
Bubacar Rachid Djaló (LIPE)	3	12,026
Joaquim Baldé (PSD)	2 (2.1)	8,623
Salvador Tchongo (independent)	2 (1.7)	6,937
José Catengul Mendes (FLING)	1 (1.3)	5,311
Mamadú Uri Baldé (PRP)	1 (0.9)	3,580
Antonieta Rosa Gomes (FCG/SD)	1 (07)	2,986
Blank votes	8	32,740
Invalid votes	4	15,647
Total	**100**	**417,992**

Source: Comissão Nacional de Eleições, 9 December 1999, 11 December 1999, and 25 January 2000.

Table 3. Results, by region and whole country, second round of presidential election, 16 January 2000 (rounded-off percentage of total vote for each of the two candidates and for blank, invalid and protested votes, total vote)

Region	Kumba Yalá	Malam Sanha	Blank	Invalid	Total vote
Tombali	66	31	2	1	25,216
Quinara	50	46	2	1	16,105
Oio	64	32	2	2	63,979
Biombo	88	8	3	2	20,398
Bol./Bij.	65	30	2	2	7,889
Bafatá	60	35	2	2	50,073
Gabú	67	28	2	2	43,423
Cacheu	81	14	3	2	44,703
Bissau	75	24	1	1	89,823
Whole country	**69%**	**27%**	**2%**	**2%**	**361,609**

Source: Comissão Nacional de Eleicôes, 21 January 2000.

Table 4. Results, whole country, National Assembly (ANP) election, 28 March 2004
(number of mandates and rounded-off percentage of total vote gained by each party)

	Mandates	% vote
PAIGC	45	31
PRS	35	25
PUSD	17	16
UE	2	4
APU	1	1 (1.3)
PU	–	5
PDSG	–	2
UM	–	2
RGB	–	2 (1.7)
PUN	–	1 (1.4)
UNDP	–	1
FCG/SD	–	1
MDG	–	1
PMP	–	1 (0.7)
PS	–	0 (0.3)
blank, invalid and protested votes	–	7
Total	**100***	**100%**
Total number of votes		**449,755**

* Two representatives of Guineans residing abroad were not elected, which explains why the sum total of mandates in the table is 100, rather than 102.

Sources: Nô Pintcha, 8 April 2004; Lusa, 4 April 2004.

Table 5. Results, whole country, first round of presidential election, 19 June 2005,
(rounded-off percentage of total vote and number of votes obtained by each candidate)

	% vote	Number of votes
Malam Bacai Sanhá (PAIGC)	34	158,276
João Bernardo Vieira (independent)	27	128,918
Kumba Yalá (PRS)	24	111,606
Francisco José Fadul (PUSD)	3	12,733
Aregado Mantenque Té (PT)	2	9,000
Mamadu Iala Djaló (independent)	1.5	7,112
Mário Lopes da Rosa (independent)	1.0	4,863
Idrissa Djaló (PUN)	0.8	3,604
Adelino Mano Queta (independent)	0.6	2,816
Faustino Imbali (independent)	0.5	2,330
Empossa Ié (independent)	0.5	2,215
Antonieta Rosa Gomes (FCG/SD)	0.3	1,642
João Tatis Sá (independent)	0.3	1,378
Blank votes	2.5	13,239
Invalid votes	2	10,516
Protested votes	0.3	1,595
Total	**100%**	**471,843**

Source: Boletim Oficial da República da Guiné-Bissau, no. 26, 1 July 2005, supplement 2; Lusa, 25 June 2005 (for party affiliations).

Table 6. Results, by region and whole country, second round of presidential election, 24 July 2005 (rounded-off percentage of total vote for each of the two candidates and for blank, invalid and protested votes, total vote)

Region	João B. Vieira	Malam Sanha	Blank	Invalid + protested	Total vote
Tombali	54	43	2	2	25,916
Quinara	38	60	1	1	17,362
Oio	45	52	2	1	60,745
Biombo	87	11	1	1	27,742
Bol./Bij.	67	31	1	1	11,819
Bafatá	48	49	2	1	58,439
Gabú	50	47	1	1	59,580
Cacheu	46	50	2	2	42,655
Bissau	49.3	49.5	0.6	0.7	118,720
Whole country	**51. %**	**46.5%**	**1.3%**	**1.1%**	**422,978**

Source: Comissão Nacional de Eleicôes, 10 August 2005.

DISCUSSION PAPERS PUBLISHED BY THE INSTITUTE

Recent issues in the series are available electronically for download free of charge
www.nai.uu.se

1. Kenneth Hermele and Bertil Odén, *Sanctions and Dilemmas. Some Implications of Economic Sanctions against South Africa.* 1988. 43 pp. ISBN 91-7106-286-6

2. Elling Njål Tjønneland, *Pax Pretoriana. The Fall of Apartheid and the Politics of Regional Destabilisation.* 1989. 31 pp. ISBN 91-7106-292-0

3. Hans Gustafsson, Bertil Odén and Andreas Tegen, *South African Minerals. An Analysis of Western Dependence.* 1990. 47 pp. ISBN 91-7106-307-2

4. Bertil Egerö, *South African Bantustans. From Dumping Grounds to Battlefronts.* 1991. 46 pp. ISBN 91-7106-315-3

5. Carlos Lopes, *Enough is Enough! For an Alternative Diagnosis of the African Crisis.* 1994. 38 pp. ISBN 91-7106-347-1

6. Annika Dahlberg, *Contesting Views and Changing Paradigms.* 1994. 59 pp. ISBN 91-7106-357-9

7. Bertil Odén, *Southern African Futures. Critical Factors for Regional Development in Southern Africa.* 1996. 35 pp. ISBN 91-7106-392-7

8. Colin Leys and Mahmood Mamdani, *Crisis and Reconstruction – African Perspectives.* 1997. 26 pp. ISBN 91-7106-417-6

9. Gudrun Dahl, *Responsibility and Partnership in Swedish Aid Discourse.* 2001. 30 pp. ISBN 91-7106-473-7

10. Henning Melber and Christopher Saunders, *Transition in Southern Africa – Comparative Aspects.* 2001. 28 pp. ISBN 91-7106-480-X

11. *Regionalism and Regional Integration in Africa.* 2001. 74 pp. ISBN 91-7106-484-2

12. Souleymane Bachir Diagne, et al., *Identity and Beyond: Rethinking Africanity.* 2001. 33 pp. ISBN 91-7106-487-7

13. Georges Nzongola-Ntalaja, et al., *Africa in the New Millennium.* Edited by Raymond Suttner. 2001. 53 pp. ISBN 91-7106-488-5

14. *Zimbabwe's Presidential Elections 2002.* Edited by Henning Melber. 2002. 88 pp. ISBN 91-7106-490-7

15. Birgit Brock-Utne, *Language, Education and Democracy in Africa.* 2002. 47 pp. ISBN 91-7106-491-5

16. Henning Melber et al., *The New Partnership for Africa's development (NEPAD).* 2002. 36 pp. ISBN 91-7106-492-3

17. Juma Okuku, *Ethnicity, State Power and the Democratisation Process in Uganda.* 2002. 42 pp. ISBN 91-7106-493-1

18. Yul Derek Davids, et al., *Measuring Democracy and Human Rights in Southern Africa.* Compiled by Henning Melber. 2002. 50 pp. ISBN 91-7106-497-4

19. Michael Neocosmos, Raymond Suttner and Ian Taylor, *Political Cultures in Democratic South Africa.* Compiled by Henning Melber. 2002. 52 pp. ISBN 91-7106-498-2

20. Martin Legassick, *Armed Struggle and Democracy. The Case of South Africa.* 2002. 53 pp. ISBN 91-7106-504-0

21. Reinhart Kössler, Henning Melber and Per Strand, *Development from Below. A Namibian-Case Study.* 2003. 32 pp. ISBN 91-7106-507-5

22. Fred Hendricks, *Fault-Lines in South African Democracy. Continuing Crises of Inequality and Injustice.* 2003. 32 pp. ISBN 91-7106-508-3

23. Kenneth Good, *Bushmen and Diamonds. (Un) Civil Society in Botswana.* 2003. 39 pp. ISBN 91-7106-520-2

24. Robert Kappel, Andreas Mehler, Henning Melber and Anders Danielson, *Structural Stability in an African Context.* 2003. 55 pp. ISBN 91-7106-521-0

25. Patrick Bond, *South Africa and Global Apartheid. Continental and International Policies and Politics.* 2004. 45 pp. ISBN 91-7106-523-7

26. Bonnie Campbell (ed.), *Regulating Mining in Africa. For whose benefit?* 2004. 89 pp. ISBN 91-7106-527-X

27. Suzanne Dansereau and Mario Zamponi, *Zimbabwe – The Political Economy of Decline.* Compiled by Henning Melber. 2005. 43 pp. ISBN 91-7106-541-5

28. Lars Buur and Helene Maria Kyed, *State Recognition of Traditional Authority in Mozambique. The nexus of Community Representation and State Assistance.* 2005. 30 pp. ISBN 91-7106-547-4

29. Hans Eriksson and Björn Hagströmer, *Chad – Towards Democratisation or Petro-Dictatorship?* 2005. 82 pp.ISBN 91-7106-549-

30. Mai Palmberg and Ranka Primorac (eds), *Skinning the Skunk – Facing Zimbabwean Futures.* 2005. 40 pp. ISBN 91-7106-552-0

31. Michael Brüntrup, Henning Melber and Ian Taylor, *Africa, Regional Cooperation and the World Market – Socio-Economic Strategies in Times of Global Trade Regimes.* Com-piled by Henning Melber. 2006. 70 pp. ISBN 91-7106-559-8

32. Fibian Kavulani Lukalo, *Extended Handshake or Wrestling Match? – Youth and Urban Culture Celebrating Politics in Kenya.* 2006.58 pp. ISBN 91-7106-567-9

33. Tekeste Negash, *Education in Ethiopia: From Crisis to the Brink of Collapse.* 2006. 55 pp. ISBN 91-7106-576-8

34. Fredrik Söderbaum and Ian Taylor (eds) *Micro-Regionalism in West Africa. Evidence from Two Case Studies.* 2006. 32 pp. ISBN 91-7106-584-9

35. Henning Melber (ed.), *On Africa – Scholars and African Studies.* 2006. 68 pp. ISBN 978-91-7106-585-8

36. Amadu Sesay, *Does One Size Fit All? The Sierra Leone Truth and Reconciliation Commission Revisited.* 2007. 56 pp. ISBN 978-91-7106-586-5

37. Karolina Hulterström, Amin Y. Kamete and Henning Melber, *Political Opposition in African Countries – The Case of Kenya, Namibia, Zambia and Zimbabwe.* 2007. 86 pp. ISBN 978-7106-587-2

38. Henning Melber (ed.), *Governance and State Delivery in Southern Africa. Examples from Botswana, Namibia and Zimbabwe.* 2007. 65 pp. ISBN 978-91-7106-587-2

39. Cyril Obi (ed.), *Perspectives on Côte d'Ivoire: Between Political Breakdown and Post-Conflict Peace.* 2007. 66 pp. ISBN 978-91-7106-606-6

40. Anna Chitando, *Imagining a Peaceful Society. A Vision of Children's Literature in a Post-Conflict Zimbabwe.* 2008. 26 pp. ISBN 978-91-7106-623-7

41. Olawale Ismail, *The Dynamics of Post-Conflict Reconstruction and Peace Building in West Africa. Between Change and Stability.* 2009.52 pp. ISBN 978-91-7106-637-4

42. Ron Sandrey and Hannah Edinger, *Examining the South Africa–China Agricultural Relationship.* 2009. 58 pp. ISBN 978-91-7106-643-5

43. Xuan Gao, *The Proliferation of Anti-Dumping and Poor Governance in Emerging Economies.* 2009. 41 pp. ISBN 978-91-7106-644-2

44. Lawal Mohammed Marafa, *Africa's Business and Development Relationship with China. Seeking Moral and Capital Values of the Last Economic Frontier.* 2009. xx pp. ISBN 978-91-7106-645-9

45. Mwangi wa Githinji, *Is That a Dragon or an Elephant on Your Ladder? The Potential Impact of China and India on Export Led Growth in African Countries.* 2009. 40 pp. ISBN 978-91-7106-646-6

46. Jo-Ansie van Wyk, *Cadres, Capitalists, Elites and Coalitions. The ANC, Business and Development in South Africa.* 2009. 61 pp. ISBN 978-91-7106-656-5

47. Elias Courson, *Movement for the Emancipation of the Niger Delta (MEND). Political Marginalization, Repression and Petro-Insurgency in the Niger Delta.*2009. 30 pp. ISBN 978-91-7106-657-2

48. Babatunde Ahonsi, *Gender Violence and HIV/AIDS in Post-Conflict West Africa. Issues and Responses.* 2010. 38 pp. ISBN 978-91-7106-665-7

49. Usman Tar and Abba Gana Shettima, *Endangered Democracy? The Struggle over Secularism and its Implications for Politics and Democracy in Nigeria.* 2010. 21 pp. ISBN 978-91-7106-666-4

50. Garth Andrew Myers, *Seven Themes in African Urban Dynamics.*2010. 28 pp. ISBN 978-91-7106-677-0

51. Abdoumaliq Simone, *The Social Infrastructures of City Life in Contemporary Africa.* 2010. 33 pp. ISBN 978-91-7106-678-7

52. Li Anshan, *Chinese Medical Cooperation in Africa. With Special Emphasis on the Medical Teams and Anti-Malaria Campaign.* 2011. 24 pp. ISBN 978-91-7106-683-1

53. Folashade Hunsu, *Zangbeto: Navigating the Spaces Between Oral art, Communal Security And Conflict Mediation in Badagry, Nigeria.* 2011. 27 pp. ISBN 978-91-7106-688-6

54. Jeremiah O. Arowosegbe, *Reflections on the Challenge of Reconstructing Post-Conflict States in West Africa: Insights from Claude Ake's Political Writings.*
2011. 40 pp. ISBN 978-91-7106-689-3

55. Bertil Odén, *The Africa Policies of Nordic Countries and the Erosion of the Nordic Aid Model: A comparative study.*
2011. 66 pp. ISBN 978-91-7106-691-6

56. Angela Meyer, P*eace and Security Cooperation in Central Africa: Developments, Challenges and Prospects.*
2011. 47 pp ISBN 978-91-7106-693-0

57. Godwin R. Murunga, *Spontaneous or Premeditated? Post-Election Violence in Kenya.*
2011. 58 pp. ISBN 978-91-7106-694-7

58. David Sebudubudu & Patrick Molutsi, *The Elite as a Critical Factor in National Development: The Case of Botswana.*
2011. 48 pp. ISBN 978-91-7106-695-4

59. Sabelo J. Ndlovu-Gatsheni, *The Zimbabwean Nation-State Project. A Historical Diagnosis of Identity and Power-Based Conflicts in a Postcolonial State.*
2011. 97 pp. ISBN 978-91-7106-696-1

60. Jide Okeke, *Why Humanitarian Aid in Darfur is not a Practice of the 'Responsibility to Protect'.*
2011. 45 pp. ISBN 978-91-7106-697-8

61. Florence Odora Adong, *Recovery and Development Politics. Options for Sustainable Peacebuilding in Northern Uganda.*
2011, 72 pp. ISBN 978-91-7106-698-5

62. Osita A. Agbu, *Ethnicity and Democratisation in Africa. Challenges for Politics and Development.*
2011, 30 pp. ISBN 978-91-7106-699-2

63. Cheryl Hendricks, *Gender and Security in Africa. An Overview.*
2011, 32 pp. ISBN 978-91-7106-700-5

64. Adebayo O. Olukoshi, *Democratic Governance and Accountability in Africa. In Search of a Workable Framework.*
2011, 25 pp. ISBN 978-91-7106-701-2

65. Christian Lund, *Land Rights and Citizenship in Africa.*
2011, 31 pp. ISBN 978-91-7106-705-0

66. Lars Rudebeck, *Electoral Democratisation in Post-Civil War Guinea-Bissau 1999–2008.*
2011, 31 pp. ISBN 978-91-7106-706-7

www.ingramcontent.com/pod-product-compliance
Lightning Source LLC
Chambersburg PA
CBHW080210300326
41934CB00039B/3444